DEER TRAILS

DEER TRAILS

Kim Shuck

San Francisco Poet Laureate Series No. 7

City Lights Books | San Francisco

Cover photos copyright © 2019 by Doug Salin

"Change" was published under the title "The Hills Hold Down" in
Red Indian Road West (Scarlet Tanager Press, 2016).

Library of Congress Cataloging-in-Publication Data

Names: Shuck, Kim, author.
Title: Deer trails / Kim Shuck.
Description: San Francisco : City Lights Books, [2019] | Series:
San Francisco poet laureate series ; no. 7
Identifiers: LCCN 2019020877 | ISBN 9781931404181
Classification: LCC PS3619.H83 A6 2019 | DDC 811/.6—dc23
LC record available at https://lccn.loc.gov/2019020877

City Lights Books are published at the City Lights Bookstore
261 Columbus Avenue, San Francisco, CA 94133
www.citylights.com

For all San Francisco poets at whatever point in the journey, and particularly for Nina, who I will miss. For Doug, because. For Dav: breakfasts, walks and incantations. Nothing happens without a community.

CONTENTS

KIM SHUCK
POET LAUREATE OF SAN FRANCISCO
INAUGURAL SPEECH

[the poet begins, wearing a band of flowers around her head]

It is always an honor to read in Ohlone territory. Always.

Now, we are very close to an old village site, and although I could not throw a rock to there, I feel fairly certain that there are at least two men in the room who could if these buildings weren't here. So that's where we are. It's important to understand that we are rooted in that.

I'm going to start by reading the work of two Ohlone poets. The first poem is by Stephen Meadows:

"Cosmology"

Generations of spiders
weave their interminable worlds
among the rough cut boards
the hay colored chronicle
of bodies in the soft light
pendants of spirit
rivaling in abandon
the acrylics and oils on canvas
that speak to me of friends

In this room
with its colors spasmodic
over fifty some years

neither the sound of traffic
nor the rotting of the walls
nor the murmuring of poems
will halt this cosmology of gems
each delicate passed over body
a bright crypt in air

This morning I was making origami jumping frogs at the Mission Education Center in Spanish, a language I don't speak very well, and now I'm giving this speech. And people asked me before I walked in here, "Are you worried?" No, I am not. Second graders who are waiting for you to make a linguistic mistake are so much scarier than a poetry audience.

So this next poem is by Deborah Miranda, who is also Ohlone. If you don't know these writers, you should. And, with great gratitude, I note both this and the previous poem are from books published by Heyday. I love Heyday Books, by the way. This is an excerpt from a poem called "Petroglyphs":

All my life I knew that I would disappear. I knew my presence here on earth was so tentative that I was in constant danger of being devoured, absorbed, vanished.

So from the time I could hold a crayon, I scribbled. I scrawled. My hand grew cramped and tired, calluses formed on my fingers from holding a pen, a pencil. I gripped my writing utensil with four fingers instead of three, used my pinky to support the others. Gripped so hard my fingers hurt but couldn't stop. Couldn't stop, because if I did, I would disappear. Everyone I loved had disappeared. I knew I was next.

[the poet removes the band of flowers and dons a Polish hat]

I've been asked a lot of questions in the last couple of weeks since I was named poet laureate, and a lot of people have spoken of me as a Native American writer, which I am. But I can't help but remember the time my mother came to one of my art shows and looked at my bio, which had been edited by the people at the gallery, and they had taken out the fact that I am half Polish. Those of you who know what they're looking at will recognize a Goral mountain hat from Poland, the Alpine Carpathians where my grandfather is from. Think the other side of the mountain: I'm from the land of the vampires. My grandfather was a union organizer for the painters union here in San Francisco. When we really, really, really remembered how to do that. When you didn't have to say you were "pro union" in this town because we all knew it.

This next poem I think you should know about is a piece by Ire'ne Lara Silva called "Blood Sugar Canto." When I was trying to write my inaugural address I found that Ire'ne's piece came closer to what I meant than anything I wrote.

I read something about American artists and their mindsets. Something which did not include me as an American—not me in this brown, Mexican, Indigenous, queer, disabled body.Something which did not speak to my art.

I forget sometimes that for some people art is a luxury, a pastime. Even for those who make art, they see it as something to chase, stealing the stories of others, seeking out experiences in order to have something to write about, pushing themselves to extremes to make themselves feel.

I forget because that's not the art I make. Not the art the people in my world make. Writing is the closest art to me, so I will say "writing," but I mean "art-making" in all its forms. In my world, we write because we must, because "no nos queda de otra," because it is how we survive, how we crawl out of self-destruction and hopelessness, how we dream, how we create ourselves, how we speak, how we believe, how we reach out to one another, how we build, how we heal—ourselves, our communities, our ancestors, and our future—how we say, over and over again, we are human… we are here…we are free.

I didn't, of course, nominate myself for this position. I was at a party actually at Heyday Books, and another poet, Kurt Schweigman, walked up to me and said, "I think you're going to be the next poet laureate of San Francisco." And I laughed at him. Then I went off to the corner to finish my aram sandwich and drink some juice quietly by myself. Somebody else came up to me that day and said the same thing. Then later, at a different event, another poet, César Love, asked if he could nominate me. I said, "Sure, and I'll even do it, if they choose me." So here I am.

What I've decided to do, during my time as poet laureate, is to make a poetry map of San Francisco. It's a project I've wanted to do for a long time. In the coming months, many of the poets present here will be tapped for poems, poems about heroes who have left us and places that mean something really important to them. Specific places, not vague places, because this city is amazing. It's an incredible place. How many of you know that we used to have a Native Elder center in Hayes Valley? This is an incredibly high-rent Native room here right now; you have no idea. There are Native people from across the continent here right now and I am incredibly grateful. When Luis Herrera said that it felt like family in this room, I almost said, "You know what? This is my family."

[the poet removes the Polish hat, puts on a rabbit hat, and tosses the ears dramatically off her face]

Those of you cheering are probably the ones who know what Rabbit stands for. I am going to end up writing about Mary TallMountain, if nobody else ends up doing so, but only because Bill Vartnaw will be writing the piece about Carol Lee Sanchez, though he doesn't know it yet. This poem is by Mary TallMountain:

"The Last Wolf"

The last wolf hurried towards me
through the ruined city
and I heard his baying echoes
down the steep smashed warrens
of Montgomery Street and past
the ruby-crowned highrises
left standing
their lighted elevators useless

Passing the flicking red and green
of traffic signals baying his way eastward
in the mystery of his wild loping gait
closer the sounds in the deadly night
through clutter and rubble of quiet blocks

I hear his voice ascending the hill
and at last his low whine as he came
floor by empty floor to the room
where I sat
in my narrow bed looking west, waiting
I heard him snuffle at the door and
I watched

He trotted across the floor
he laid his long gray muzzle on the spare white spread
and his eyes burned yellow
his small dotted eyebrows quivered

Yes, I said.
I know what they have done.

Since I've been named poet laureate, reporters have been asking me things, like "Why do you write?" I think I've covered that. I always want to ask people, when they ask me that, "Why don't you?" Because I don't know how to do it any other way. Similarly, I've been asked things, almost surreptitiously, like "What's it like to be Native American?"

Now, for clarity, this isn't something I learned how to do later in life. To me, that question always sounds like, "What's binocular vision like?" Or "What's how bipedal locomotion like?" I don't have an answer. "What's it like to be you?" I don't know that either. I will say this: being Tsalagi, for me, is knowing that I am loved because whenever I need them, my family shows up. Do you see them all here? Look around you.

Five years ago, my daughter died. People asked me how

I kept going, and I would answer it with these people, who carry part of my sadness for me. That's how. And that's what it's like.

Carol Lee Sanchez did a lot of things for me. Among them, she introduced me to devorah major, in a roundabout way; it didn't happen directly, but it happened in that poetry way. And without devorah, I wouldn't have been able to pay my bills the last couple of years. She's had me substituting for her and got me some teaching work. She's always been supportive. Thank you, dev. It's an honor to be in your footsteps up here.

This poem is Carol Lee's, it's from a section called "Notes from San Francisco" from an incredible book called *From Spirit to Matter*:

"the song: the dance: the poem"

1.
i toil in the field
syllable into line
through the breath.
the breathing is difficult
the birthing.

i dreamed of you   mama,
far away, talking hours
into the night.
the breathing was difficult
and you changed again
trying to tell me something

I couldn't remember—except
the field was there and
stretched on and on.

the stubble would not
be replaced with new corn
and spring is soon.

the breathing is
difficult at times
from syllable into line.

So why am I wearing a rabbit hat? Rabbit is the trickster god
for the Cherokee People. Or the Trickster Spirit, depending on
who you talk to. Rabbit haunts me, so I figured I'd bring him
directly, so I wouldn't get swamped by him.

The first thing that happened after it was announced
that I had been named poet laureate was that somebody
contacted me and asked me if I identified as LGBT. I am in
my 50s. People have found that an amusing puzzle since I
was 14. I don't answer that question anymore, because there
have been a lot of different answers to that question and I am
not currently interviewing for the position of "lover," which
means that there are three whole people on the planet who
need to know who I personally feel like snuggling up with at
any given time; they would be, when important, my doctor,
my partner, and I. I already know the answer. My partner is
taking another picture of me right now. And I don't think my
doctor is here.

So I answered that question the way I have for a while.
I have a number of flippant answers, because really, it's no-

body's business. The way adults usually deal with this, rather than asking, is to look, make a guess, and keep it to yourself. But, I said, "No, not really," because "No, not really." Then somebody printed that I was evasive and did not want to go on record. So I'm going to go on record about a few things.

[the poet removes the rabbit hat and puts on a San Francisco Giants baseball cap]

I'm in my 50s, Cherokee, Goral Polish, and a baseball fan. I don't really want to say what team because I don't want to play favorites or anything. And I'd go to more games if I could figure out how to trade a poem to get in.

[the poet doffs the Giants cap and replaces it with a San Francisco Seals cap]

Generally monogamous. Omnivore. Still have my own teeth.

[the poet replaces the Seals cap with a purple giant squid hat]

I am the kind of person who believed in the giant squid before they found one. And because I actually think Lee Francis would have found this funny, I'm going to read a poem of his with the giant squid hat on. This is from Lee Francis' book *On the Good Red Interstate*:

Nyah Carol

I try to keep you in present time
            message bringer woman

disconnect you from a common past
                    guitar playing poet
build boxes for all my memories

                    San Francisco nights
                            skipping down telegraph hill
                    Santa Fe evenings
                            drinking with movie stars
                    Cubero mornings
                            climbing sandstone rocks
                    Washington daylights
                            looking at monuments

I still wear the shirt you made last year
                    artist drawing mentor
greet each day with a smile
                    mother and grandmother
place memories in little boxes

                    Santa Monica
                            swimming in the ocean
                    Albuquerque
                            walking city streets
                    Sausalito
                            listening to John Handy
                    San Fidel
                            playing kick-the-can

I pass the fifty to you again
                    horse rider Capricorn

spend quiet moments alone
        entertainer teacher
add memories to little boxes

        Corrales
            where Lewie always played
        Fairfax
            talking all night long
        Las Vegas
            hoping to change reality
        Seal Beach
            sharing our grief and pain

I visit a thousand planets
        counselor companion
consider well your message
        Oak clan cousin sister
stack boxes logically in order

        Red
            for sun and passion
        Blue
            for water and rest
        Green
            for earth and action
        Yellow
            for corn and change.

[the poet removes the giant purple squid hat and dons the band of flowers again]

Let me tell you about this city.

I'm wearing this band of flowers because it's part of the story. This was made for me by my nursery school teacher, who's here tonight and who's known me since I was three years old. I had her until I went to elementary school, where I was one of the early people in Ruth Asawa's Alvarado Arts Project. After elementary school, I went to junior high, where my best friend's mother was Kate Wolf, the singer/ songwriter. I dated Carol Lee Sanchez's son. Carol Lee introduced me to California Poets in the Schools, where the next person I am going to read was a big mover and shaker.

This poem from *No Easy Light* by Susan Sibbet is called "What It Will Be Like":

A mistranslation from César Vallejo

I will live in a city with walls made of light, of water,
where the tender fuchsias are never thirsty.

I will live in a city made of intricate wires and sand,
a city without flying paper or Kleenex,
a city of bread.

In my city the crusts will be chewy, sour—
golden stucco and brown shingle—
the heel of the loaf will be the curve of Land's End.

And in this glass of air
and clouds, my city will be dazzling, especially
when the light slips under the fog,
just before the glittering night.

The hills will be made with the bones of houses
And the gulls will fly up silently at night
The only one awake will be my small black cat,
And his song will be so beautiful,
No one will ever be sad again.

I have had the best education in art, and in having a good heart, that anyone could have. I'm not pretending that it's over. I am going to read one piece from Tongo Eisen-Martin. This is from his first book, *Someone's Dead Already*:

Waiting for Prints

Like weapon is to jacket and precinct hold Friday hostage.
Fossil Jaw then Judge

Tunnel at the end of the light
See an overtime hurricane smacking more houses

> sleep
> until
> woke by
> dry
> cereal
> and
> surrend
> —er

This holding cell only needs a giant pan handler's palms
To shake these coin men around

The man is a genius. I fully expect to be sitting in the audience when he's standing up here doing this one of these days.

It must be made clear am a Californian and a Native. I am not a Native Californian Native. My people are from the other side of the continent. In Europe this is how I explain it: it is as though you went to someone in Prague and asked about the Troubles in Ireland. I have studied them but I have no special insight.

This River

Runs west and
Counter to every story I drank
Deep in those small doll days
Strange, heavy with collective
Unconscious with all of those
West running, improbable relations spending
Lavish hands worth of emotion on this imagined
West in this city which also
Runs west into an ocean that I
Own no stories for, borrowed ocean full of
Marvels fed by these long men who collect different
Water who polish stones that won't tell me the
Future in any language I know

I want to say, even though they've been acknowledged already, that I personally as a writer, as an artist, as a human being, have received some gift in the words of every one of the people who has been a poet in this city, a poet laureate before me in this city. I am a product of my time in this place.

DEER TRAILS

Navigation

Hard to tell if this is
Fog or
Prayer smoke and the
Singing of flowers and
Horns already in
Some places these poems
Wisping into snakes and some
Dissolving going
Who knows where or
Falling into the dark of
Buried mirrors

Change

Try to dream the things that
Yerba Buena plants dream when the
New printed storm runs
Fingers through the
Cypress and reaches
Along hidden
Roots and quiet water songs in the
Cracks in the serpentine they
Find salamander prayers in layered
Stone
Coins lost in the fret of
Post earthquake with
Slumped brick and the
Full panic of
Witness and dynamite these
Hills hold down hold
Down and breathe
Storm and
Smile up into the
Rain eyes and
Change again

Cusp

Morning star the
Redwood has caught her for the
Moment this
Ancestor net this
Old game on the cusp of a day that I
Know will be hot will
Bake the tiny tomatoes on the
Vine and
Set the lavender and
Rosemary scent
Free
Ripples of early
Autumn that
Break out in
Orange butterflies

Saved

Feast of all souls prepared with the
Bones of the dead the
Packed memories of a family who
Presses flowers and saves
Recipes and skies and the
Tips off of shoelaces this is a
Sky I might save fold into a
Fortune teller with its bands of hot pink with its
Echo of a phone call from the
Disappeared mythical
Cousin because anything at all is
Possible at any moment I will
Carry dice from now on, develop a
System of predictions based on soup and
Crackers and replace latches on the
Doors of a house in a
Storm that selectively pries at the
Deepest secrets to reveal that they are not
Where we left them

Immeasurable

Fog in earnest and
Here near the
Mint and
Candle flowers the
Songs of
Seep and absorb call
Quicker feet could
Become that smell
Lemon thyme and
Rosemary before they
Cut the redwoods down these
Fogs would be combed out
Less than a mile down the road
West there maybe there is a
Stump to navigate by an
Abbreviated tooth of
Wood and ghosts they
Knew something those
Tall cousins a thing about
Ancestral blood and
Ravens and
Sea fog
Immeasurable by
Victorian or
Pythagorean tools a thing that is
Also not the sipping of
Wild pink roses

Contraband

No need to
Forbid the songs on a
Monday morning with the
Cold
Shivering the lights near the
Mint and the
Braced grey buildings with their
Red blinking
Signals to airplanes
Beware
I think of a
Fortress as an
Old-fashioned thing and in a way it is but we are
Not singing and the
Barricades are up in some
Pretense of offense the
Boats have entered the Bay and the
Songs are not being sung although we are
Allowed and
Revolution is a tea or a
Jacket and does not lend
Support and still the
Streetlights are
Trembling as the
Woman under them
Does not and we will measure her
Worthiness for help her

Parents and her
Choices and the
Mess the
Bold fact of her there and she isn't
Singing either not soup or
Poem no
Song of any kind

Tensioned Thread

What risk will you
Feed in the quiet hours in the
Winter hours? I am
Assured that there were no
Bees in the Americas before the
Invasion but there is a Mayan
God of bees and I
Wonder if it isn't the
Bee version of the
Empty new world I
Wonder if beadwork inspired by
Knotted rugs was a communication
Between Native women and
Kazakh rug makers the
Knots and beads a
Code that didn't translate into
Words but some other magic that does not
Feed us but
Fills the mouth with something other than
Words
And if that could happen then
Why not a smile as well why not
Invest in these
Quiet messages we send each other we
Send ourselves?

The End of the Drought

Panic is a luxury for those
Who are only in danger
Seasonally
Relax between battles
Some people don't want your
Smile or help
Don't want you in the neighborhood they have
Chosen from a catalog
There is a heat that only comes from these sidewalks
Nowhere else
I can only sleep with my head on the shoulder of a
Cousin these days
Perilous I understand
Explain to me
What is safe
Away from this kitchen table
Texture and quality of your words and
We weave
Weaving time is here
Sift
Pull
Edit
Manage
Stand with me now
In the ceremony of living
By breathing water
The rain is coming

Relax between battles
Smile or help
there is a heat that only comes from these sidewalks
What is safe?
Weaving time is here
Manage
The rain is coming

Wishing Fog

Blank page of heavy
Fog the
Drawing in of this
Weather the curled
Cat of it the tea
Steam the soft
Sweater whispers
Suggestions to the
Wishing fog and
Tumbles softly into
Such a day

Under Foot and Sidewalk

Among the tall ships
Wrapped tight in earth now north east
Towards the
Recreated waterfront
Teacup full of
Atmosphere
Charming
Historical
And the singer holds the mic so you can sing along
We know all of the words
Foghorns signal so that you can
Avoid bumping into people
Their tents on the sidewalk
An unsightly need that could make you feel
Almost human
These ships remember ocean
Tight quarters
Sweat and sway
Some days they tremble
Riding waves of imagination
We made believe and made
Real
These bricks as solid as anything
Things being what they are
Could burst into moths
Or shrouded restaurant tables in
Narrow streets

Palmful of
Seeds that
Every newcomer thinks they've discovered
I myself have been discovered in every decade of my life
Try not to break too many dreams on the rocks
On the tentpoles
It can take a moment to get your footing

Only When You Are Here

I miss you when you're here
Some afternoons peeking
Through the lens at
Images of Southport and
Every other thing is fine but the
Pictures of a place I've never been
Make me cry
I only miss you when you're here this
Week they're singing songs about
John Lennon we have to get more
Careful more careful your
Details are perfect and the
Dirt smells of
Thursday's rain
I miss you so much when you are
Here because I am here and the
Geometry is strange in the offhand way of
Houses that grow in
Spirals over years and the funny
Put away toys that we look at but
Don't play with don't
Ever play with

The 43

Afternoon busses
Glide up Monterey like quiet weather a
Promise of fog on the south hills and that
Preacher bird is telling it straight from every fence post and
Rooflet and I whisper to him
"Teach"
Mended gods look out from every hipshot house and storefront
What do you believe in?
The city presses palms flat against the thought of
Afternoon winds and has a brief fantasy of creeks

Arroyo Dolores

Ghost arroyo
Filled in but
Digging
Redigging
Sad creek never ran
All year and now so frail we
Feed her water
Mouthful by mouthful we
Feed her our
Ravenous sister under the
Full moon
November moon that
Also fills the ghost
Wash ghost water
Glowing back glowing
Back and guarded by bay
Laurel roots that have
Found her and we feed her
Mouth and mouth of water of
Light of
Root

Please Tell My Family I'm Alive

It's hard to know where we are with
Everything broken and
Scattered
War and weather will do that and there's
Weather to come we
Need to decide what we all understand and what is
Local

Survived like a single teacup

Always strange what's
Spared and what's
Taken the chair has
Come apart and roof pieces mixed in
With spilled sugar that
Horrible quilt of your
Mother's is ok

Storm sound has marked me I'll never stop hearing it

Shocking now the idea
Safe as houses and we did
Feel safe we
Did pull our
Ideas around us like the
Wooden walls and we thought we
Knew

Stump of the Navigation Tree

Ritual morning orange red behind the
Cypress and
Rose tea you and your
Skies you are here with me
Now these two days of
Endless words careful
Words the stump of the
Navigation tree invoked
Yesterday
Trees are
Vertical rivers trees as
Magicians and I may need to go
Touch what is left to
Ground that idea to let that
Idea flow back because it's
Far too much for this morning and its
Shadows and blue that grow
Sharper by the second

Click

These are the mists right to the
Road the chase for some the
Revelation for others this
October moon and all of its
Promises hissed into a
Crazy wind or
Brushed by crow wings over
New bridges over
Rumpled ideas of this
City baked
Apple sugar and
Dried berry poems
Printed on the bus
Or blinked in
Patterns one
Person to another and the
Season clicks over clicks
Over in all of the
Muscle and planning of
Harvest

When I Grow Up

The gate was not proof against
Prayer shawl weather
Clinging with passionate nails to the
Grass or sweeping over the museum
Running palms along the neck and arms of
Chilled bronze and
Weaving the pillars together I can see you with your
Fog light hair and
Glitter shoes feet planted wearing
Trails of alabaster moisture like your own personal
Ornament I sat there by the fountain
Stunned and watched you
Dance something wild and old
Something I wanted to touch the heart of that
Uncompromise that overjoy and with
Such sure toes and
Loving fingertips

Coming Down into Eureka Valley

This hillside remembers being wild and the
Trees still talk about the orchard that replaced
Purple bunch and
Rattlesnake grass the
Arroyo
Salamanders coil under ceramic pots and
Sing songs about wet years under the
Bay laurel and the
Yerba Buena explain the
Fog and how the
Hillsides came to be
White roses grew from a rootstock after the
Grafts failed and the
Bearded iris bolted
Every ten years or so saffron crocus
Bloom
Under mirabelle plums

In Monterey

Before the reading I watch the
Bats orbiting
Courting there are
Fat moths here to catch the
Hunting is good the bats remind me that the
Hunting is good in
Culver City we tuck ourselves in and
Listen to the thunder there is
Thunder and the
Crickets and at least one frog sing along
The hunting is good

Dangerous

I have put my
Body in dangerous places and
Wasn't being my
Father's daughter dangerous?
Traveling in possession of a
Womb and a brain crumpled
Bits of understanding and
Expectation hidden under the
False lining of these shoes a
Willingness to
Walk with my sisters to sit
Not quiet but
Talking in among the beans
Seeds or plants passed
Hand to hand the
Unpublished poems
Whispered to dried sage
Leaves and handed on in hope
Assata you are my
Relative my teacher a
Woman in danger as we all are in these and
Other times a woman whose
Face is on a poster whose
Registered fingerprint can be
Waved can be
Called up we were not meant to
Live this long were none of us

Meant to live this long endangered
In danger
Dangerous

Old Games

Should we call this
Rain? Here just down from the
Crest of the hill the
Water rarely stops me it
Rarely changes plans I want to
Chase pea shell boats down the
Gutters to the
Drains there is enough just now to
Lift boats even as light as this there is
Enough

Artichokes and Jade Bones

We run along the coast our
Kid feet still wet with
Willingness we
Run alongside the
Staccato rails that
Vanish and appear in
Tufts of indigenous
Shrubs and stands of weed
Eucalyptus we
Strawberry and
Artichoke we
Chase flotillas of
Brown pelican and
Dance to our own childhoods
Of beach and driftwood not
Replanted here but of this
Strange and colonial
Place so
Surface patchwork but the jade
Bones show the tossed
Stone chewed to cheese by olive
Mussels it's a
Generous place if
Sometimes sleepy and this
Fog sings old songs too

Force

It must take force to break a
Spirit
We've been finding pieces of you for years in
One another the
Tight curls behind an ear the
Set corners of your mouth that
Streak of green in a left eye the
Fanged eyeteeth we know you again
When we see them
Our autobiographies are written
Somewhere else by
People who have never eaten at our tables or
Picked stones for
Leg rattles that we are expected to
Pose in for the
Book covers they
Practice our signatures and sometimes even we can't tell
Houses are always
Puzzleboxes there is an
Order to things a
Way to the very center our
Softwood floor never
Finished the
Patchwork of doorknobs and step creaks
What force it must take

Blackberries Getting Ripe

Mourning doves have gathered on the roof ridge
Across the way
Odd year for the plums only about
Two hands full the year peels off in
Irregular polygons and it's just
Possible that there isn't a song for this
Sort of afternoon the
Mourning doves are planning up there on the
Blue house in soft productive
Syllables these houses are holding out
Holding up the old
Arroyo is quiet but the
Bay tree is whispering
Dark green the bay tree is
Whispering green and green irregular
Polygons that
Somehow fit together and then we will have a song we
Will have a song then

Abalone

Lady of rain combs her hair on the east bay hills
Calm for the moment
Abalone arranged
Small
Precious
Chunks of
Windshield glass
A spell
Strung as a necklace
Tomorrow she may tell us a story
We will wait

Watershed

Village sites still sing
Resonate through hidden
Shell mounds from every
Watershed that
Wrap the hills on thick aired
Nights like these
Songs throb through the
Sidewalks through the
Bark of
Bay trees in the ache of
Full bloom and
Every angled slab of rock
Peering through the
Hillsides around Rocky Point and
Glen Park Canyon remember their
True names and
Call them out like
Birds do
Announcing boundaries
Unseen but heard if listened for there is still
Joy in these hillsides the
Water still runs here

Like Grown

Let's go dance a
Fall invocation into the
Beach sand just where the
Cliffs and their attendant
Rocks provide punctuation let's
Dance until we are dusted like
Spice drops and salt stings on our
Skin lets dance the
Butterfly migration and the
Tayberries along this
Marveling coast and then dance the
Spaces between
Fantastic things dance
Every hug and oregano plant and
Sun warmed wood deck with the
Periodic condor overhead let's
Dance fiercely like the grown
Women we are

Celebration

 Arts of destruction
They built new temples on the
Footprints of the old on the
Water systems they didn't understand from the
Stones of grander buildings until they
Crumbled themselves or
Wandered off to
Pillage something else in this
Light the
Swings at the playground in the
Park the
Play houses at the zoo the
Old pool by the beach I can
See them all
Can taste waffle dogs the
Hot of beach sand in the '60s
On days like this I pull my quilt of
Sidewalk squares around me

Hey John
for John Trudell

Look at them play love like a
Word find game play
Politics and there along the
Creek the people are talking story in
Patterns and rhythms with the
Water who is trying her best to love us
John, it's raining again in
San Francisco the clouds come close
Come in and we're talking about islands in the
Bay online they are
Selling a treasure map and the
People are whispering love to the
Small rocks and scattering them on the beach
One morning can change everything, John, one
Morning of press and fret
Song and threat I can hear you from here I
Can hear you from then if I sit on the
Porch you know the way
There's an extra plate
One way and the other
People are here to make sure other people are fed

Dav

Who will help renew the spells now?
Weeks were when life was a dance with
Steps a beat you could hang a
Hat on
Limits that would hold
Rainwater or
Burning coals with equal
Reverence
A counted number of
Prayers and the
Birds live in the tree up the hill they are
Talking to me
Sitting on the roof to
Open peanut shells as the
Weather shift comes in on a
Chill wind it would have been a good Sunday to
Walk

Drag Out the Old Gloves

Play catch with me
Let's
Drag out the old gloves
Mine a mold of a decades gone version of this hand
Healing percussion of
Ball a
Rhythm a
Known weight and size
Play catch with me
Sweat polished leather conjuring
Afternoons out back with
Grandma
Pulling weeds to the transistor sputter of
Giants games and then maybe a half hour of toss and
Thud
Her lazy and
Perfect gesture the
Ball quick
Here in the midsummer hill fog
Play catch with me and draw the spirits
Baseball ghosts whispering possibility
Singing songs of grace and ungrace
Surprise and striving
When the day is too perfect for the usual
We can fall into a whisper of
Baseball
Float on a memory of

Baseball or something close
Walking past stories of
Seal Stadium the
Vibrations catch me in their unfaded spectacle
As we drive by
Kezar or
From the airport along the bay edge where
Candlestick birds still flock
Love me in this year and season
Play catch with me

For a Moment Grey Wolves Are Back in California

Oh what it takes to
Smuggle grey fur back
Into this place to
Birth these scraps of
Story here in this far
West this dry
West to birth them
Damp in the crackle
Grass on these hills to
Sing to the gasping trees with relearning voices and
Caress with a
Snarl of new
Fur of
Grey fur and
Curious
Cautious frog
Chasing
Guardians are back they are
Back and gathering

Safety of Streets

If you fell as rain on this
Hillside
Squirrels might eat you as
Plum petals they
Fall
Cupped like small
Palms at the foot of
Diamond Street the
Eucalyptus might make
Seed pods out of you
Grown in the shadow of
Whimsy and
Rescue finches the
Sound of the
Model railway in your ears
Two hills over you might just
Catch Mary's poems in your
Web of linked
Oxygen and
Hydrogen
You might
Know the streets of Norton and Bummer we are
Grown too serious the
Man read a poem about the safety of the
1800s when my skin might have been
Sold to the state for a bounty define
Safe sing me a song of

Rainwater and
Supermarkets
Sing me a song of rain and
Neighborhood
Fall with me like
Rain

Over the Roots

Up the hill a raven
Flying into the fog flying
West into the
Backlit fog
Wind coming in over the roots of the
San Francisco and
San Mateo railway over the
Roots raven wings
Pacific fog coming in towards the
Bay
Here between the hills in
Among the hills where the land
Snugs down when the land
Crouches down
Raven wings
Facing the afternoon sun

Standing in the Dark by the Back Door Window

There are days when I wear you more
Surely than the handed down strands of
Coral stolen when I was still a
Child and the
Visions get clearer in these smaller
Days the
Butterflies have made it up this far
I tell you the
Rain brought you out this morning as we
Approach your birthday it would have been
Ninety-eight of them this year I found another
Box of your treasures in the
Closet as if
Every shovel full of exploration finds more of you and they've
Strung the holiday lights again we'll
Look out the kitchen window tonight we'll
Look at what used to be your city

Such a Thing as Rebuilding

This is the
Fourth morning the ravens have
Joined me at dawn
Adding their quiet mumbles to my
Quieter
Singing
Soft sweater echoes the
New red in the east
Feathers reflect everything and
Maybe these are the
Obsidian shards we are meant to
Bury to lead the dead
Either way they leave them for me
Under the lichen ridden plum trees
Between bricks
Slumped from the ''o6 fire
Yes there is such a thing as rebuilding and
Under the roots
Just here the
Arroyo ran to the
Mission
Wrap the sling cord around the crown of your hat
Sit here with me and the
Birds they say
Rain on
Saturday
We can wait together

Wonders

Just here at dawn
Who says that wonders need to be rare the
Redwoods are the first here to start their long inbreath
Days are a sequence of similar curves and we
All sing water the
Bay laurel is swelled with nuts
Throws chemical poems into the
Old creek bed
Fog is trying
She's trying

Migration

Community vivisected
Brick by poet
Business by
Burned building the
Student's father died in the
Fire and we're getting into
Boats or walking
North because there is
No reason to stay and what
Remains are memento mori
I can barely breathe for your
Death
Pick an unlucky number my
Birth caul was buried in that place the
Tree they planted over it still
Stands and sometimes
Kicks out an
Apple that will squeak against the press of
Teeth as you bite a
Cousin stayed an
Auntie
Stubborn as gathering
Kindling she ties
Spell knots near the market
Because we can't bear the sight we
Leave because we won't
Let it all die out we stay the language

Stretches to gauze it
Pulls and prickles and
Holds still a word like
Understanding always comes first in the
Old sounds a word for
Dumpling the
Song my grandma bounced me to
Refugees that found a place
Ah ah ah the knee bounces the
Fuss of the old bakery the rattle of words

People

This town isn't the skyline it's the
Roofline it's the
J line out in the flats and memory of
Playland
This town isn't the
Gate it's the
Stairs we leapt to avoid a
Childhood fantasy of rising lava the
Pavement under roller skates
This town is ghost orchards
Piped creeks
Unmarked graves and
Unremembered villages
This town is things in the beach sand
Low tide
Fort Point in a
Thundering fog
This town is necking in the van behind the
Conservatory of Flowers the
Eucalyptus slow dripping on the windscreen a
Particular coastal code
This town is people
Past and present it's
The people, the people
We're the people

Spin

Pollen shower and
Ripe peaches this
Breath this one
Moment and the next and
No
Everything isn't this
Spin and dance and light but I
Try to be brave enough to see
Those things when they
Whisper colors to me on a
Warm afternoon
There is always time for
Mourning and I will
But the
Wild eternity keeps
Singing

Market Street/Hibernia Bank

Nothing extra in this city not the
Abandoned bank in all of its
Neo-classical self-confidence or
Shattered bottle lenses in
Any color but
Rarely green or clear because we
Aren't as wild as reports suggest
These funny angles have seen a few things
Some of them white gloved ladies in careful hats
Because sacred regalia takes all kinds of shapes
You know this is a neighborhood too
Even gone the way it has
Social lace of drawn threads the
Structure tenuous a
Formal tablecloth we save for best
Fragile
More and more with each
Tradition clipped and
Carefully pulled from the fabric
That restaurant an empty storefront
Used to be a birthday tradition
Across the street was
Saturday breakfast

To Know the Local Songs

Old habits become
Superstition
Walking through
Puddles to confuse the dogs the
Favorite bench for
Squirrel feeding even though it's
Not allowed now the one near the pond
Growing up during the 70s drought taught that
Days the rainbow falls were on could be
Lucky something about the
Choreography of water the
Hypergraphia on the remains of the
Sutro baths that spun
Useful history out over the sea wall
Conjured the city your family knew
Wet concrete will
Tell you things too when the
Heat spins the hydrogen and
Oxygen into that
Unexpected windless air it's
Uncommon in these
Flexed October afternoons and the
Union Square fountain will
Whisper and some of those songs are ours too

Exuberant

Rain calling me with mumbles and a
Variety of
Warm colors like
Expensive flowers and I'm
Not trying to guard my
Sanity anymore
Every bit of packaging stripped is
More bubble wrap dance to
Share I'm
Not guarding my
Sanity these days and this rain with
Coded messages tapped on
Roof and window a
Language I have to keep learning this
Chenille morning with fog and
Burgundy and tangerine songs that will
Stick in your curls
Don't sing me so loud I've
Stood down the guards it's just this
Cruel pink and dusty lacquer red
Taps and hisses to decode the
Weather and the murmels and
Mumbles we decide to
Hide in a
Drawstring bag that we may well
Carry everywhere

Headstones

That you might be a word like the
Feel of huckleberries on my
Tongue the shiver and
Strange harmony of it that you
Might be those longed for fall
Afternoons and the
Visit to
Butterflies the
Breakfast diner and all that
You might be a drive over that pass the
Headstones that say
Limerick in marble carved by hand and by
Rain that you might be the
Lemon and basil smell that
Clings to my hair today that you might
Breathe for me

Cannibals

They will only be silent when they are distracted
Cannibals
Life feeding on life
Want to be allowed where they don't want to go
Want to rent furnished lives
Scattered with objects of witness and
Remain untouched
Want exotic words without context
Want to know without understanding
Want to be where they are not wanted
The ceilings didn't need to be this high and the
Sunrises here will take your breath away

Egret Tree in Williams

Back and forth of
Nestling care
Fill the spaces between roads
Improvised weaving
Because people like paths
Because sometimes there are reasons for them in
Apple country
Blackbirds chat
Fluid dynamics
Theoretical math
Baseball scores
Blackbirds in numbers like
Ritual
People like roads up through the pass
Mountains singing hot afternoon to a star the
First star a planet but
Spirit dogs eye the seed corn and make
Plans
Pathways
Creek bed to
Crest
Take possession of what they can't
Keep
Spill story

Ritual

Today I'm burying words in jars
Under the bay laurel
Snuggled between plum
Roots
Word preserves in
Jars for
Quieter times I'm
Burying her words for when her words
Run thin or stop she
Knows some things so I'm
Saving them nothing like the poems of
Summer abandon because that's a
Thing to find
Each for each
Because wonder is a practice a
Prayer or whatever you like to call it but these jars
Now they are a real thing
Maybe a recipe for
Beans or fish or
Biscuits that no one else can follow
Something very time and person specific
Like any good religion

Generations

Grandma left me a bag full of lost answers
Puzzle pieces a never-identified snapshot a
Wedding ring but I don't ask the right
Questions all of the watches run
Strange they run strange but the
Borage seeds sprouted
Flew into blue dazzle in the summer and
Reseeded along with the single
Hollyhock the cineraria and the
Pot marigolds
The glass vanity jars smell of
Evening in Paris and all of the
Tiddly Winks are in the box but there are
No houses in the
Monopoly set and we're out of
Yatzee cards

Field Trip

Point of shift
Sand to
Foam to
Headstone I
Remember the
Taravel tunnel it
Comes in dreams and
Memories of
Field trips and
Quilted coats
Honey sandwiches gone transparent
They're running the old L trains down market these days
Cars slip between
Effigies of a west
Made safe
Known
Until the
Sand shifts again the
Fog shifts again

Sinew and Marrow

Heartbreak sky with the
Fog badly dyed streaks of
Red and I can
Taste the apples but also your
Mouth and every sweet thing there is to
Know those moments of
Understanding so deep they drag at
Sinew at
Marrow the way that I knew in that first
Conversation that you were a thing that
I wanted to learn

Feathers and Pavement

Shattered mirror of feathers and
Pavement I am hunting
Hunting the sweet
Calamity smell of burning wood the
Cooper's hawk perfumes his feathers cuts
Through the smoke and the
Ravens run close behind but
They already smell of fire
Burning
Gnaw of
Burning burning did you know us before the
Disaster before the
Feathers and psychopathy we are not poems of the
Dissatisfied we take our
Songs to the edges and let them play in the
Mother fire

Lancet Eye

Deep thoughts of ravens can
Change you the
Dark of the feathers sure but that
Lancet eye the
Meteor burn of them will paint on your thoughts
What's the pinecone for?
Rabbit whispers from
Eastern marshes
Whispers in shapes with
Irregular angles the
Shapes fill with this
Western fog as
Solid as I remember the
Kind we haven't had and I can
Show my sons how to stir the fog
Show them what to look for
there are no
Answers just stunning shapes and a
Considered moment

Santa Rosa or Twin Pines

Sometimes the fires become visible and the
Response teams come there are
Firemen and water is delivered by helicopter
In the end the
Burnt trees stand
Dark with char dark with
Fire that can be touched can be seen and then
Quiet flames in the walls of the houses the
Thoughts of the powerful they
Take out more than under growth
Silent fire that
Sears idea and
Idea twisting in
Ignored corners the places we
Forget to look and the
Sometime minor flares and the
Every so often
Let the embers build let the
Possible spread until the
Visible disaster
Returns and is blamed for everything

Burned Out

Fall cooling
Old buildings
Friends
Wearing their finest
Charred boards
No cast off nesting material for
Newcomers but
Lives and a
History of lives pulled
Hot
Through the hands and minds of
Current neighbors

Thumbnail Wings

Little blue butterflies with
Thumbnail wings and
Rattlesnake grass the
Perfect mud green
Salamanders with their
Tiny fingers
The mica in the dirt on this hill
Glittered from the rocks too
Sour grass and bay laurel nuts with their
Sharp skins
Bunch grass and
Sedge root and small leaf
Sage
Sometimes we'd see a
Garter snake playing dead in the leaves
Sometimes catch a bullhead on a single hook line in the
Bay the children of the
War were still singing in the
Streets their long hair
Unalloyed personal perspectives
Beginning to swell and bloom
I found a
Jack ball at the foot of the church stairs

A Prayer for Dancing

Recent full moon and I
Want to wake up hearing the
Weather report from
Port Arthur or
Somewhere else that didn't know it was
Making history the dark is claimed by specific tides
Transformation and wet air and this morning draining
Pulling west with
Songs from Sausalito and
Texas clicked like switching tracks the
Trains still run here still
Mumble love songs to the
Rails and what's love if it isn't
Careful mapping
Kind measuring come awake to the
Weather report from Port Arthur the
Windshed over the coastal hills here the
Coastal sage knows in leaf vein and
Stem that it's a prayer for dancing

The Baths

There are maps that you have to keep
Singing since they
Hauled the doors of the
Ruin away we start there in an
E minor and the
Quiet deep pools and the
Globs of melted glass
Statues on that hill and the
Crazy light on the clouds we are
Singing maps and light on the clouds the
Small crabs freeze if you look at them no matter how many
Private jets
There are cracks in the rocks
We stood there and
Skipped flat stones into the
Surf knee deep in
Cold water we
Stood there in
E minor and sang so that we would
Remember if you hold the singing up to the
Crazy cloud light you can see it
Can see my city whole

Old Monterey Road

Poems are the cure
Sounds that
Rumble bones like a purr
Invocation of the
Red edge of a storm cloud over the
San Gabriels
Poems are the prescription
Taken at dawn near water or
Leaning over to tend the music in a car
Car headed
North headed to the
Draped pistachio trees the
Morning fog that soothes like
Poems unfolded and
Rustled into the air along the old
Monterey Road
Strawberries and old wineries the
Working bars the
Railroad tracks set at the level of
Fifty year flood water
We can be healed
We can be made whole

After Sunset

Lights on the hillside
Expensive as they are
Lean in towards the eye's fingertip
Maze me as totally as
Ridges on turtle scutes the
Complicated wonderful the
Treasure the drive from Corta Madera in the dark
Across the Bridge that has shaken more sturdy
Imaginations than mine
Blown like raven down to
Stick on these
Metal/salt weavings the
Shiver accent of
Bay wind from Miwok to
Ohlone across the gate

Deer Trails

The streets are not just streets they are the
Thoughts and intentions of people who
Lived here before have
Left marks have
Named
Thought prints guide
Trade paths
Deer trails the
Shadows of bird migration the
Picking out of a way a
Good way without too much mud or
Dirt slip this path is a
Gift
Travel grateful
Travel safe

Kim Shuck is an Ani Yun Wiya (Cherokee)/Polish-American poet, author, weaver, and bead-work artist who draws from Southeastern Native American culture and tradition as well as contemporary urban Indian life. She was born in San Francisco, California and belongs to the Northern California Cherokee diaspora. She is a member of the Cherokee Nation of Oklahoma. She earned a B.A. in Art (1994), and M.F.A. in Textiles (1998) from San Francisco State University. Her basket weaving work is influenced by her grandmother Etta Mae Rowe and the long history of California Native American basket making. She is the winner of the Diane Decorah First Book Award from the Native Writers' Circle of the Americas and the Mary TallMountain Award for Freedom Voices. She is also one of 13 recipients of the Academy of American Poets inaugural Poets Laureate Fellowships.